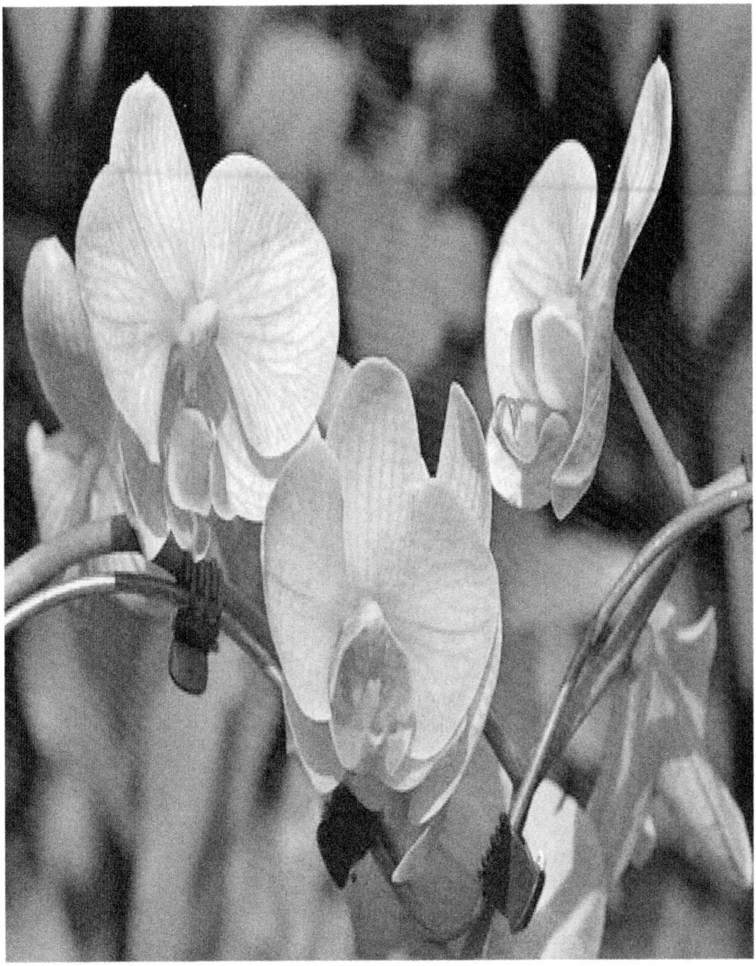

GROW YOUR ORCHIDS

Ultimate Guide on how to Grow, Care and water your orchids flower perfectly to a full bloom.

MICHAEL GRONNY

Copyright 2021 Morgan.

This book is subject to copyright policy. All rights are reserved, whether the entire or component of the material, particularly the right of transformation, reprinting, recycling illustration, broadcasting, duplicating on microfilm, or in any other way. No part or even the whole of this book or contents may be produced or even transmitted or reproduced in any way, be it electronic or paper form or by any means, electronic or mechanical, also include recording or by any information storage or retrieval system, without prior written permission the copyright owner, **Morgan LTD.**

TABLE OF CONTENTS

INTRODUCTION 7
PART 1: SHOPPING FOR YOUR ORCHIDS FROM THE FLOWER SHOP: 9
FULL-BLOOM ORCHID: 10
TIPS TO LOOK AT FOR BEFORE BUYING ORCHID: 12
USING A WIGGLE TEST: 13
ORCHID ROOT NETWORK: 14
ORCHID LEAVES: 16
GROWTH BULBS OF THE ORCHID: 16
UNOPEN BLOOMED: 17
PART 2: STEPS ON HOW TO GROW ORCHIDS 18
STEP 1: SELECTING A SPECIFIC SPECIES OF ORCHIDS: 19
STEP 2: SELECTING THE BEST KIND OF SOIL FOR YOUR ORCHIDS. 22
STEP 3: POTTING MIX WITH DIFFERENT SIZES 24
STEP 4: CHOOSING A SNUG POT FOR YOUR ORCHID: 27
POT YOUR ORCHID: 29
STEP 5: KNOW WHEN TO RE-POT YOUR ORCHID: 30

STEP 6: REQUIRE TEMPERATURE LEVEL: 31
STEP 7: LEVEL OF SUNSHINE NEEDED: 32
STEP 8: WATERING YOUR ORCHID ONCE IN EVERY WEEK: 34
STEP 9: ORCHID CARES: 34
STEP 10: THE USE OF FERTILIZER: 35
STEP 11: MAINTAIN THE HUMIDITY LEVEL: 37
STEP 12: UNDERSTAND THAT ORCHID PROCESS ARE DIFFERENT: 37
PART 3: TYPES AND SPECIES OF ORCHIDS 38
Terrestrial orchids: 39
Epiphytes orchids: 40
Epiphytes Orchid grows on trees: 42
PART 4: CARING FOR ORCHIDS: 45
ATTENTION THAT YOUR FLOWER NEEDS: 46
SUNLIGHT LEVEL: 47
TEMPERATURE LEVEL: 49
WATERING LEVEL: 50
FERTILIZER LEVEL: 51
PART 5: HOW TO WATER YOUR ORCHID 52
SUPPLY OF WATER: 52
TROPICAL AREAS AND HUMIDITY LEVELS: 55
WHEN YOU OVER-WATER YOUR ORCHID: 56

PART 6: ORCHID ARTIFICIAL LIGHTS METHOD 58
LEVEL OF LIGHT REQUIRED FOR YOUR ORCHIDS: 59
SUNNY CONDITIONS: 60
ARTIFICIAL INDOOR LIGHTING FOR ORCHID: 61
PART 7: ORCHID AIR CIRCULATIONS 65

INTRODUCTION

Orchids have rapidly proven as one of the most common house plants. Orchid comes in a variety of species and hybrids. They are not difficult to grow if you give them the right amount of water, sun, fertilizer, and air. Although certain orchid species prefer colder temperatures, some thrive in temperatures ranging from 75 to 85 degrees Fahrenheit.

Orchids are the world's most diverse plant family. With 30,000 species to choose from, you can buy a new orchid every day for eighty years and still not be able to develop them all.

Back in the real world, readers of this lovely book will be able to rapidly and easily identify the orchids that seem to be right for them, such as those that will grow on a windowsill, those that require artificial lighting, how to care and water orchids. This book is suitable for beginners and also intermediaries. You will also learn to determine which species within a given class are the best, to begin with, once you have chosen your orchid.

PART 1: SHOPPING FOR YOUR ORCHIDS FROM THE FLOWER SHOP

So you have opted to take care of orchids – That is great to hear; You are one step closer to having a tropical-style garden at home, with a complete variety of orchids in full bloom but before you go for orchid purchasing, read our procedures to ensure that you get a healthy orchid that will bloom gorgeously during the growing season.

FULL-BLOOM ORCHID:

Sometimes some orchid growers do ask; should we buy orchids that are already full-bloomed?

A fully bloomed orchid appeals to the large percentage of first-time orchid purchasers since it adds immediate beauty to any garden – the flowers are already present to them. However, if you buy an orchid that has already bloomed, keep in mind that some varieties, such as the phalaenopsis, create so many flowers that they are unable to regain for the next blooming season.

Orchids can produce flowers until they die, as a result; experienced orchid growers, as well as enthusiasts, may believe that an orchid in full bloom is an orchid on its way out. So be worry if you are offered such orchids.

TIPS TO LOOK AT FOR BEFORE BUYING ORCHID:

The followings are essential tips you need to look for before you buy an orchid.

USING A WIGGLE TEST:

Using a wiggle test is very essential. This is simply by holding the plants close to the roots and shake them in right and left directions to see whether it will sustain their stand. Ensure you shake it gently.

The wiggle assessment can be used to check orchids such as cattleya as well as brassavola, and also dendrobium. What if you notice some roots poking through the potting material close to the top?

This is fine as long as the plant as a whole appears to be strong and thriving. You can still consider purchasing the orchid if the potting appears to be inappropriate or inadequate, you can still consider buying it as long as you repot it once you get home.

ORCHID ROOT SYSTEM:

The root system of an orchid is by far the most essential part of the plant. The orchid's complex root system is essential for anchoring it to the pot as well as transmitting moisture, minerals, as well as other nutrients - rich from it.

When roots are relatively dry, they usually appear light green. Roots can turn a dark green color when wet. If the orchid's roots are tan (or light brown) or white, it may be nearing the end of its life cycle.

ORCHID LEAVES:

The orchid's leaves, in addition to its roots, are critical to its sustainability. Ensure that the leave is not soft, no blemishes also glossy leaves and slightly yellow-green leaves are good.

GROWTH BULBS OF THE ORCHID:

It's time to examine the orchid's growth bulbs. The growth bulbs are the endpoints from which new stems, as well as flowers can emerge.

Some orchids, such as the phalaenopsis, only have one growth point. Others, such as the cattleya plant, grow from elongated rhizomes. When purchasing new orchids, always inspect the bulbs for healthy and plumpness (the latest bulbs are referred to as "pseudo bulbs").

UNOPEN BLOOMED:

Avoid orchids that have already bloomed entirely if you want to cherish your orchids for a longer period, Orchids with some open buds as well as some closed buds are good choice because you will be able to see them bloom in the coming weeks.

PART 2: STEPS ON HOW TO GROW ORCHIDS

Orchids are one of the most attractive flowers in the whole plant world, mixing exotic appearances with a varied range of attributes. Orchids are beautiful plants, containing over 30,000 individual species including over 200,000 hybrid different type of orchids one of the second biggest families of plants in the world.

Orchids are certainly peculiar. However, they are hard to develop effectively mostly indoors as well as outdoors for any possible green thumbs. Someone who hope to grow orchids should brace themselves both for the mistakes and triumphs brought by the breeding of this beautiful species.

The followings are steps on how you can grow your Orchids:

STEP 1: SELECTING A SPECIFIC SPECIES OF ORCHIDS:

Few orchids are easier to grow than many others. Cattleya, Phalaenopsis as well as Paphiopedilum orchids are one of the simplest to grow and therefore are recommended by most inexperienced gardeners including orchid growers. However, it is estimated to be over 40,000 species of orchid species — that is two times the number of existing bird species and four times the amount of existing mammalian species.

Phalaenopsis, Dendrobium including Oncidium is perhaps the most popular kind of orchids for sale. The group Dendrobium has about 1,200 species of orchids and seems to be a classic orchid epiphyte; the Oncidiums are distinguished by column wing as well as a callus on the floral lip. It is a classical orchid, which is known as the 'moth orchid' and it is highly popular with beginners.

Various orchids generally have various ideal moistures, increasing temperatures, watering schedules as well as light specifications. Talk to your local orchid growers or visit your orchid community's local section to find out what made your orchid species most valuable.

STEP 2: SELECTING THE BEST KIND OF SOIL FOR YOUR ORCHIDS.

Most of the time orchid growers make the mistake of choosing the wrong kind of soil for orchids. Using the kind of soil that is not suitable to grow orchids will kill it or make it not grow properly.

Most of the time many orchid farmers make use of sphagnum moss with or in combination with coconut shucks as well as charcoal, Perlite, and sometimes even Styrofoam pellets as a potting mix.

STEP 3: POTTING MIX WITH DIFFERENT SIZES

Ensure that you use the proper pot size for your orchids. If the orchid is large you can use a medium or large size pot.

Make ensure that you keep the moisture more than most by:

- Creating or buying a suitable potting mix that is most convenient for miltonias, oncidiums, and small size roots.
- Ensure that one part perlite. One part grain fir bark.
- 4 parts fine (grain) coco husk.

MEDIUM POTTING:

Creating a suitable medium potting mix that are cattleyas as well as phalaenopsis including other mature orchids. Most of the time growers who are not sure of what to use sometimes go for a medium-grade potting mix. The fine grade mix is 4 medium (grain) grain fir bark, 1 part medium charcoal, and 1 part perlite.

STEP 4: CHOOSING A SNUG POT FOR YOUR ORCHID:

Several orchids thrive in a root-bound environment. Choose one potting medium for your orchid, and make sure there are more than enough drainage holes in the pot itself. Try and stay away from decorative pots and also, as the glaze is toxic to orchids. Recognize that over-watering is often the enemy of orchids. Longer pots are required for some orchids, including such cymbidiums, to accommodate their long root systems.

The common categories of pots are an alternative to the traditional clay pot (which is what most orchid gardeners accept also prefer):

- Total combined pots with wire mesh enable a more absorbent ecosystem. For healthier sunlight,

these could be hung in strategic locations.
- Clear plastic pots allow more sunlight to reach the roots. These enable the gardener to examine the root systems of the orchid without disconcerting it.

- Wooden pots with rot-resistant wood construction. Before putting your potting blend in any wooden pots, line them with layer moss.

POT YOUR ORCHID:

Cut off any dead as well as rotting roots before removing the orchid from its initial pot and also before putting the plant inside its pot, divide the root matter up into multiple segments if necessary. The most mature segment of growth should be placed near the pot's bottom, while newer growth should be placed near the pot's sides. Apply a thin layer of potting mix to the root system, barely covering it.

STEP 5: KNOW WHEN TO RE-POT YOUR ORCHID:

In the broad sense, you will have to repot your orchid mostly every two years or whenever the lower leaves of your orchid begin to die. If your orchid outgrows its pot or even the roots are dying, you might have to repot it.

STEP 6: REQUIRE TEMPERATURE LEVEL:

Majority of orchids are common in tropical and subtropical climates, which means adequate ventilation, plenty of light, as well as 11-15-hour days (365 days a year).

The temperature ought to be between 60 and 80 degrees Fahrenheit (obviously it depends on the orchid species) (18.3 to 23.8 degrees Celsius). During the fall and winter, lowering the temperature of the orchid's surroundings by about 10 degrees at night will encourage new buds.

STEP 7: LEVEL OF SUNSHINE NEEDED:

Several orchids prefer oblique sunlight; direct sunlight causes them to burn, while insufficient sunlight causes the plant to die. Position your orchid near a window that faces south or east. A west-facing window may receive too much light, while a north-facing window may receive insufficient light.

If you want to know if your orchid is receiving too much or too little light, look at its leaves. The leaves of an orchid ought to be light green with yellowish undertones. Dark green leaves indicate that the orchid is really not getting sufficient light. If the leaves are yellow, brown, as well as reddish in color, they are overfed.

STEP 8: WATERING YOUR ORCHID ONCE IN EVERY WEEK:

It's simple and easy to kill an orchid by overwatering, it is better to underwater it. This will enable your orchid to dry out but water it once a week. Longer days but instead much more heat during the summer months may necessarily require a shorter watering duration. Enable your orchid to dry out by watering it for 15 seconds and afterward placing it on a tray of pebbles.

STEP 9: ORCHID CARES:

Orchids necessarily require far more care than the average plant or flower. The thicker your leaves are, the more probably it is that your plant will need more water. Less water is better if your plant has bulky faux-bulbs. Orchids aren't particularly difficult in most situations, but they are when it comes to water consumption. Again, they grow well with a water shortage than with an excessive quantity of water.

STEP 10: THE USE OF FERTILIZER:

For better output, it is better to fertilize your orchid once every week with a weak (20-10-20) fertilizer mixture or combinations (diluted to 1/4 or 1/5 strength). Then, once every month, water the flower with clean water to remove any accumulated fertilizer.

If your fertilizer is too much, you risk burning the roots as well as preventing the flower to grow properly; if you fertilize infrequently, you risk hindering the flowering system. Maintain the plant in the shade until the flower spike appears. Brace the spike with a tie-up when it's about 6 inches (14-16 cm) tall.

STEP 11: MAINTAIN THE HUMIDITY LEVEL:

Maintain the humidity of your growing room. The reason because wherever it is — at about 58 percent to 80 percent at all times, due to orchids' natural affinity for humidity. You can achieve or accomplish this level by placing trays of pebbles with water near the orchid or by running a humidifier near the orchid.

STEP 12: UNDERSTAND THAT ORCHID PROCESS ARE DIFFERENT:

Each orchid species has its own set of procedures and it requires a certain level of care. Every orchid is unique, requiring a distinct temperature, lighting environment, as well as watering schedule. As a result, when choosing an orchid plant to grow, you must be flexible.

PART 3: TYPES AND SPECIES OF ORCHIDS

Despite the fact that orchids come with a wide variety of species as well as hybrids.

There are currently two kinds of orchids:

Terrestrial orchids:

These are kinds of orchid species that grow on the ground. Perhaps one of the most common orchids are terrestrial orchid species while terrestrial orchids have roots like many other plant species, grow below the surface of the soil, some terrestrial orchids are semi-terrestrial; therefore, have both aerial as well as underground origins. Cymbidium orchids are ground orchids with 40 species including a thousand hybrid species. They were one of the first orchid species to be grown.

Epiphytes orchids:

Epiphytes orchid grows on trees, rocks, and poles. they are the other kind of orchid. In reality, the word epiphytes are not reserved for an orchid. It applies to any plant with an overground root system. The most recognized orchid epiphytes are dendrobiums while quick to grow, they take a little more care than Cymbidiums and therefore do not flower regularly.

More than 1000 of them are species. They can be seen in northern India, Southeast Asia, Australia, and Polynesian natural tropical environments. Dendrobiums flourish in a wet, and humid environment, and Phalaenopsis is another common form of epiphyte of the orchid.

These orchids have long-lasting flowers and therefore are easy to grow. They can be used in multiple colors, such as pinks, yellows, and sometimes even skateboarders, sometimes at a wedding.

Epiphytes Orchid grows on trees:

Structures like trees are dominated by epiphytic orchids and if they grow up on the tree, they are not fed by the tree. They settle down on branches and bark of trees by their fleshly roots. As nutrition for the plant is used on the organic compounds that settle between roots as well as branches. The plant can be sustained by epiphytic orchids during wet and dry times.

The rough stringy base is covered by a spongy layer that can quickly trap water. This cover soaks water as it rains. It turns light green when fully saturated. The roots of the orchid hold moisture and eventually release it into the tissues of the plant.

Few epiphytic orchid species often stick to rocks. The epiphytes grow in filtered light and therefore are suspended from trees or rocks in open, oxygenated conditions.

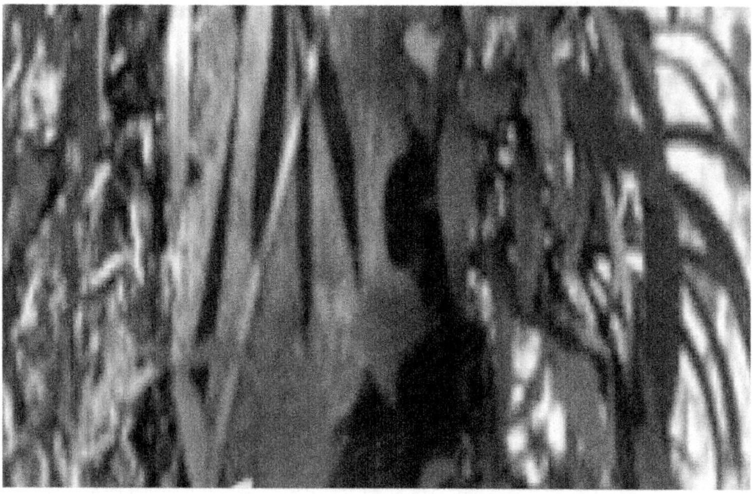

PART 4: CARING FOR ORCHIDS:

For a long time, numerous people believed that having to care for orchids is challenging. It is only for the superwealthy and privileged people With over 30,000 species as well as 150,000 hybrids.

Anyone can discover an orchid that fits their environment, budget, as well as a baseline of horticulturist skill.

The followings are things you need to put into considerations:

ATTENTION THAT YOUR FLOWER NEEDS:

The majority of orchids do not need a lot of attention like every other house or garden plant. However, some orchids have specific characteristics. Finding out what your orchid require is the first phase in orchid care and must always be your priority. Orchids are one of the few plants that can generate such a delicate as well as lovely bloom. It's one of the reasons they are such a widely known house plant.

You can maintain your orchids blooming to look healthy and fit as they were in the store if you take excellent care of them. A phalaenopsis is a common orchid that you may have received as a gift or purchased from a store. This is the widely known white or purple orchid plant that is accessible because it is extremely easy to care for than some of the less prevalent orchid varieties.

SUNLIGHT LEVEL:

If orchids are properly care for they will bloom for at least 4 months. Your orchid should be placed near a window so that it can get plenty of light throughout the day. However, you should avoid direct sunlight during the day, as it can be too harsh for these plants, but instead consider giving your orchid morning as well as evening light.

As a result, the eastern part of your household is an ideal location for your orchid. You can use fluorescent lights to replace natural sunlight if you place them about a foot above the orchid's flowers, but you should still minimize access to daylight hours.

TEMPERATURE LEVEL:

Orchids survive in temperature levels above 55 degrees Fahrenheit but still below 80 degrees Fahrenheit. Orchids that are exposed to temperatures above 90 degrees lose their buds as well as stop blooming altogether.

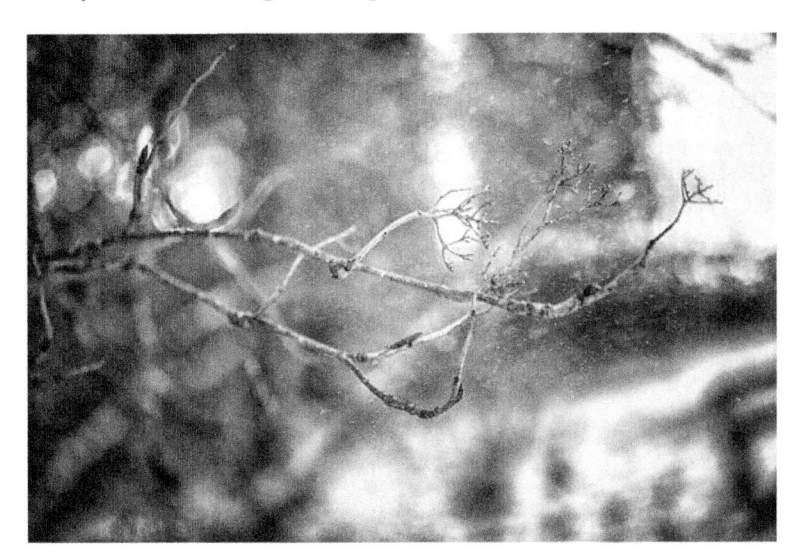

WATERING LEVEL:

It's important to keep the flower wet, but don't overwater the roots as this will kill the orchids. Instead, Regardless of weather factors, the scale of your orchid container plays a role in determining how much you can water it. A 6-inch pot requires water every 7 days, while a 4-inch pot requires water every four to six days. maintain it in a water tray all of the time. Make sure the roots do not come into contact with the water tray, or it will continuously soak up too much water.

FERTILIZER LEVEL:

Fertilizing the orchid before it blooms is a good way to make sure that it stays in bloom as long as possible. It is no longer necessary to fertilize it once it has bloomed. Another piece of advice for maintaining your orchid in bloom for as long as possible is to cautiously prune the orchid when it is in bloom.

PART 5: HOW TO WATER YOUR ORCHID

Because of their beautiful blooms and a wide range of species, colors, also sizes, orchids have rapidly become a favorite among houseplants. Orchids, like any other plant, need the right environmental conditions to flourish.

SUPPLY OF WATER:

Trying to give your orchid the proper volume of water is an important part of providing the best growing conditions for your orchid because the quantity of water needed by different orchid species varies, it's essential to do some research on your specific plant. However, knowing about orchids in particular and also where they come from is beneficial.

Providing your orchids with water is an easy route to humidify them. A depth saucer, as well as some pebbles, are available for orchid owners. The pebbles should be poured into the saucer. Place your orchid pot on top of the saucer's pebbles, after which water the pebbles. Make sure that the water does not come into contact with the orchid pot itself. You can develop a unique high-humidity climatic condition around your orchids by doing so.

TROPICAL AREAS AND HUMIDITY LEVELS:

Orchid plants are most commonly grown in tropical and subtropical climatic conditions around the world. There is a lot of rain in the areas where there are a lot of orchid plants. In their natural habitats, they can be very warm and moist. In fact, most orchid plants prefer a humidity level of 80 percent given that in a room with an average humidity of 80%.

WHEN YOU OVER-WATER YOUR ORCHID:

Overwatering is among the most essential things to know when trying to care for your orchids. Some owners conclude that if the potting soil appears to be dry, the plants require to be watered. This is untrue when it comes to orchids. Even though the potting bark appears to be dry it retains moisture. Water your orchid plant sparingly once a week or every other week, according to the general guideline.

When continuing to grow orchids in your home, make sure the potting bark is dry before watering them. Orchids grow on tree stems and leaves in some species. It's common for their roots to dry out in their natural habitats before being re-watered.

PART 6: ORCHID ARTIFICIAL LIGHTS METHOD

Orchids, like several other types of indoor plants, have very precise lighting, water, as well as nutrition requirements. The type of light that your orchid plant receives is one of the most significant aspects of its health. The quantity of sunlight required by an orchid plant varies depending on the species. Orchids, on the other hand, are native to tropical regions of the world and require a lot of diffused light to thrive.

LEVEL OF LIGHT REQUIRED FOR YOUR ORCHIDS:

To know how much shade as well as sun your particular orchid species requires, you will need to learn everything you can about that orchid species. There are a few different ways to get the information you need about your orchid plant. Talking to the people who sold you your orchid is a great way to learn more about it while you are researching which orchid species would be best for you, you should also search for information about your orchid internet.

SUNNY CONDITIONS:

Several other orchids require a lot of sunlight to survive while other orchid species. On the other hand, will wilt if they don't get enough shade. There are two methods used by orchid growers to determine which orchids prefer a lot of light. Orchids with a soft growth habit thrive in shady areas and sunny conditions.

An orchid that mostly prefers a soft, as well as shady growth environment, will usually provide its owners with a flourishing plant, but the blooms will be small as well as infrequent. Orchids grown in harsh or sunny conditions, on the other hand, will generate a lot of blooms but not a lot of plants.

ARTIFICIAL INDOOR LIGHTING FOR ORCHID:

Using a grow light is another way to ensure that your orchid receives the proper quality of light. You can simply buy a grow light and use it with a timer to give your orchids the right volume of energy light as well as darkness.

You can also use fluorescent light to provide your orchids with a light source that isn't too harsh for them. For years, it was thought that only accomplished horticulturists could successfully grow orchids. Orchids can now be grown by even the most inexperienced growers but thanks to these simple methods for providing the right kind of light you need to grow your orchid indoor.

Sometimes, orchid growers prefer to position their orchid flowers close to the window for easy access to the natural sun.

You can always have a stunning orchid plant that should give you a stunningly beautiful view, full blooms throughout its blooming season with natural sunlight, a grow light or fluorescent lights, and a thorough understanding of the species of your orchid.

PART 7: ORCHID AIR CIRCULATIONS

Whether you have more or less than twelve(12) orchids grouped around each other, an electric fan should be placed nearby to focus on improving air circulation all over the plants. The less air circulation in an indoor or room, the worse it becomes. the orchid is more highly susceptible to dehydration if there is no enough ventilation around the environment.

Orchids are air plant species, this means that they really ought to breathe to stay healthy as well as regulate their internal moisture levels.

If an orchid is well-ventilated, it can withstand higher temperatures caused by the direct absorption of sunlight.

Printed in Great Britain
by Amazon